Journey to Freedom

BOOKER T. WASHINGTON

BY DON TROY

"MORE AND MORE WE MUST LEARN TO THINK NOT IN TERMS OF RACE OR COLOR OR LANGUAGE OR RELIGION OR POLITICAL BOUNDARIES, BUT IN TERMS OF HUMANITY."

— BOOKER T. WASHINGTON

Cover and page 4 caption:
Booker T. Washington in 1908

Content Consultant:
Kira Duke, Education
Coordinator, National Civil
Rights Museum

Published in the United States of America by The Child's World®
1980 Lookout Drive, Mankato, MN 56003-1705
800-599-READ • www.childsworld.com

ACKNOWLEDGEMENTS

The Child's World®: Mary Berendes, Publishing Director

The Design Lab: Kathleen Petelinsek, Design; Gregory Lindholm, Page Production

Red Line Editorial: Holly Saari, Editorial Direction

PHOTOS

Cover and page 4: Bettmann/Corbis

Interior: Bettmann/Corbis: 5, 9, 27; Library of Congress: 6, 22; North Wind Picture Archives: 8; Courtesy of Hampton University Archives: 11, 12; Frances Benjamin Johnston/Library of Congress: 13, 14, 20; Corbis: 16, 17, 18, 25, 26; Cornelius M. Battey/Library of Congress: 21; AP Images: 23; Frances Benjamin Johnston/Corbis: 24

LIBRARY OF CONGRESS CATALOGING-IN-PUBLICATION DATA

Troy, Don.
  Booker T. Washington / by Don Troy.
      p. cm. — (Journey to freedom)
  Includes bibliographical references and index.
  ISBN 978-1-60253-118-5 (library bound : alk. paper)
  1. Washington, Booker T., 1856–1915—Juvenile literature. 2. African Americans—Biography—Juvenile literature. 3. Educators—United States—Biography—Juvenile literature. I. Title. II. Series.

  E185.97.W4T762 2009
  370.92—dc22
  [B]

                              2008031927

CONTENTS

Chapter One

FAMOUS WORDS, 5

Chapter Two

BORN A SLAVE, 8

Chapter Three

TOWARD TUSKEGEE, 13

Chapter Four

INTEGRATION OR SEGREGATION? 17

Chapter Five

CRITICISM OF THE
"ATLANTA COMPROMISE," 21

Chapter Six

IN TERMS OF HUMANITY, 24

Time Line, 28

Glossary, 30

Further Information, 31

Index, 32

Booker T. Washington became a national spokesperson for the black community.

Chapter One

FAMOUS WORDS

ooker T. Washington had an important speech to give. It was 1895, and he was about to become the first black man to speak in front of a southern, white audience. He needed to speak in front of a crowd of whites and blacks without offending either race.

Even though slaves in the United States had been freed 30 years earlier, blacks were not treated equally, especially in the South. **Racism** and **discrimination** still existed. Living conditions of blacks were often worse than those of whites. Blacks had lower-paying jobs and poorer housing. The inequality led to racial tension. In 1895, Washington was invited to speak on the topic

Booker T. Washington working on a speech at his desk, around 1900

of race at the Cotton States and International **Exposition** in Atlanta, Georgia.

Washington wanted his speech to address two things: the condition of blacks in the South and the relationship between blacks and whites. He knew he wanted to talk about how blacks deserved equal treatment. He wanted to say that the two groups should be able to work and live side by side. However, these were sensitive subjects at that time. Many whites did not believe blacks were their equals. Whites might become angry if Washington spoke about the need for **integration** in the South. Washington understood this.

He also understood how wonderful freedom was. Washington was born into **slavery** and freed when he was nine years old. As a young man, he realized the cruelty and injustice of slavery. He believed that black people's freedom was more important than immediate equality with whites.

With these thoughts, Washington chose to speak about the importance of work and labor as a way to improve life for both whites and blacks. He called upon both groups to use labor to improve business in the South. He did not speak about integration. In time, Washington believed that **segregation** of blacks and whites would end as a result of hard work by both races.

Washington's speech, which became known as the "Atlanta Compromise," was praised and debated. Many whites liked the speech because they wanted to continue segregation. Some blacks, however, believed Washington did not make a strong stand for black rights. His speech became famous and is regarded as one of the most important speeches in U.S. history.

Booker grew up on a Virginia plantation, where he lived in this small cabin with his mother, Jane.

Chapter Two

BORN A SLAVE

ooker T. Washington was born on April 5, 1856. His mother, Jane Burroughs, was black, and his father was an unknown white man. Booker and his mother lived on a **plantation** in Virginia. But they were not there by choice. Jane was a slave, which meant she belonged to the plantation owners as a piece of property. Children of slaves automatically became slaves too. This meant Booker was born a slave.

At that time, slavery was a common practice in the southern United States. African people were captured. They were then taken to North America on overcrowded cargo ships. Many of the slaves died either while resisting capture or during the long journey. When the survivors reached North America, they were sold at auctions. Farmers bought the slaves to work in tobacco and cotton fields or to do other hard labor.

Under this system, slaves had no rights. They could be bought and sold at any time. They could not leave their masters, no matter how badly they were treated.

In 1861, when Booker was five years old, the Southern states, including Virginia, tried to **secede**, or withdraw, from the United States. The South wanted to form its own country called the **Confederate States of America**. For the next four years, the North and South fought the U.S. Civil War.

Slavery was a part of the United States since the first colony at Jamestown, now Virginia, which was established in 1607. Slavery was introduced there in 1619. For nearly 250 years, slavery was legal in the United States. The Thirteenth **Amendment** *finally outlawed slavery in 1865.*

Even after slavery ended, former slaves continued to pick crops on plantations.

In 1865, the Confederate Army surrendered. The Confederate states rejoined the **Union**. The Thirteenth Amendment outlawed slavery throughout the nation. Booker and his family were free.

After the war, life was difficult in the South. Many farms had been destroyed in battle. Many farmers had been killed. Starting over was challenging, especially without the free labor of slaves.

Life was particularly difficult for freed slaves. Plantation owners could not afford to hire them. Little work was available, and few slaves had been taught any job skills. Finding food, housing, and clothing was difficult.

During the war, Booker's mother had married Washington Ferguson, who had escaped from slavery. When the war ended, Booker's family moved to Malden, West Virginia, and lived with Ferguson. Booker worked hard in the salt and coal mines with his stepfather and brother.

Booker had always wanted to learn to read. But slaves had not been allowed to go to school. At age ten, he pleaded with his parents to let him attend a new school for former slaves. His parents agreed.

Booker was an outstanding student. At 16, he left his school to attend Virginia's Hampton Institute. It was a college for black students. At Hampton, students could work to pay for their education. Booker worked as a janitor. He later said, "I had to work late into the night, while at the same time I had to rise by four

Hampton Institute was approximately 500 miles (805 km) away from Booker's family home. In order to attend the school, Booker made most of the trip on foot. Because of this distance, Booker was separated from his family while he attended Hampton.

At age ten, Booker attended school for the first time and quickly learned to read.

On Booker's first day of school, students were asked to stand and give their full names. During slavery, some slaves only went by their first names. This is why Booker did not know his last name. He gave his stepfather's first name—Washington—as his last. After that, he was known as Booker T. Washington. Later, his mother told him she named him "Booker Taliaferro."

o'clock in the morning, in order to build the fires and have a little time in which to prepare my lessons."

One of Hampton's goals was to teach students the dignity in working. Booker learned to love work. Years later he would say, "I have had no patience with any school which did not teach its students the dignity of labor."

Hampton taught students to count on themselves. Booker learned it was important for blacks to have the skills that would let them live independently. Booker believed people should be able to count on themselves for the things they needed.

Booker was an outstanding student at Hampton Institute in Virginia.

Chapter Three

TOWARD TUSKEGEE

fter graduation, Booker T. Washington returned home to Malden to teach at the local school. Four years later, the head of Hampton Institute invited him back to the college. Washington was put in charge of a new educational program for Native American children. He also taught night classes for people who had to work during the day. Both programs were successful.

In 1881, a white banker and a black community leader from Tuskegee, Alabama, invited Washington to start a school for blacks in their town. It seemed like an excellent opportunity. Washington decided to take advantage of it. It turned out to be one of the most important decisions he ever made.

Students working in the print shop at Tuskegee Institute, 1902

When Washington arrived in Tuskegee, he was surprised to learn that there was no classroom for the new school. But that did not stop him. He visited nearby towns to get students. He found some blacks who had already learned to read and were now teaching others. He invited these self-made teachers to be his students.

Shortly after, a local church donated a run-down shack. Washington began teaching in the old building on July 4, 1881. With 30 students, Washington could now teach young blacks the importance of relying on their own skills and abilities. Tuskegee Institute was born.

Washington decided to teach English and math right away. Many other schools taught subjects such as Latin, Greek, or philosophy. Washington decided that these would not be the best subjects for Tuskegee students.

In his visits to the small Alabama towns, he saw too many black people who were poor and hungry. What they needed most were food, shelter, and good jobs. Washington's first concern was to make sure his students could find work to support themselves. He vowed that Tuskegee would teach practical subjects on growing crops and building houses. Food and shelter, he believed, must come first.

Washington soon expanded the school. To afford the land, he borrowed half the money from Hampton Institute. Volunteers held festivals and church suppers to raise the rest.

Building the new schoolhouse was a good way to educate Tuskegee students. They learned how to dig clay, form bricks, and bake them in an oven. The bricks were heavy. Washington added classes on how to make wagons and wheelbarrows to carry the bricks. The school also needed furniture. So the students learned carpentry and upholstery skills.

Some students grumbled that they had come to school to study, not to push wheelbarrows full of bricks. But when they saw Washington shoveling clay and chopping wood alongside them, they followed his example.

At Tuskegee, Washington insisted on teaching students the importance of discipline and personal cleanliness. He believed that cleanliness helped gain respect and social acceptance. Tuskegee students had to bathe and brush their teeth every day.

Washington's family life during this time was painful. He had married his childhood sweetheart, Fannie Smith. She died just after giving birth to their daughter, Portia. Later Washington married a teacher, Olivia Davidson—but she died after having two sons, Booker Jr. and Ernest.

Being a single parent was a difficult responsibility. Washington married a third time. His new wife, Margaret, helped him provide a wonderful home for his children. Washington spent much of his time teaching, running the school, and raising money to keep the school going, but he was still devoted to his family.

Booker T. Washington spending time with his son and grandson in 1915

Chapter Four

INTEGRATION OR SEGREGATION?

n 1895, Washington became the first black person to speak to a white audience in the South. The occasion was a great exposition—the Cotton States and International Exposition in Atlanta, Georgia. Special exhibits were brought to Atlanta from all over the country. Philadelphia sent the Liberty Bell. Boston sent a model of the home of poet Henry Wadsworth Longfellow. California set up a mining camp.

Eager to encourage the North to do business with the South and to show that the Civil War was long behind them, the organizers invited Washington to speak.

It was important that Booker T. Washington deliver the right message at the exposition in Atlanta.

Washington was a confident speaker. He carefully prepared his speech for the exposition. There was a great deal he wanted to say about the racial and labor situations in the South. Although blacks had been granted certain rights after the end of the Civil War, their lives were still difficult. Many whites refused to see them as equals. Most areas of the South had segregation laws that kept blacks and whites apart. Blacks could not attend white schools or live in white neighborhoods. They could not serve on juries or marry whites.

There were frequent acts of violence against blacks as well. Some blacks watched as their homes were burned down. Others were beaten or killed merely because of their skin color. Whites who committed these crimes were rarely punished.

Washington hated the segregation laws and knew they were wrong. He knew that blacks were being denied their rights. He wanted to change this as much as possible. Yet he recognized that one speech would not convince the South to change its laws. Washington did not want to seem like a troublemaker to his white audience. He was convinced that if blacks were educated and held jobs, they would achieve success and respect. Segregation would disappear as whites began to see the contributions of blacks. He decided that segregation could be tolerated, for now, in the hope of gaining education and jobs for the black community.

In his speech, often called the "Atlanta Compromise," Washington said that it would be "extremist folly" to argue for **civil rights** at the present time. Blacks should be patient and concentrate first on education and jobs. Washington compromised by asking for less than blacks truly wanted in the hope of achieving part of their goals.

Many southerners in the audience had worried that Washington would use this speech to attack the segregation laws. They applauded loudly when he implied that segregation could be tolerated. The South had been struggling financially since the end of the Civil War. Southerners knew they needed blacks in their workforce. Yet they were not willing to give them social equality in return.

Many northerners had considered putting money into southern businesses but saw racial tensions as a danger. They, too, applauded Washington's ideas.

In a memorable moment of the speech, Washington held his fingers apart above his head. He said, "In all things that are purely social, we can be as separate as the fingers." Then he closed his fingers into a fist and added, "yet one as the hand in all things essential to mutual progress."

The speech made Washington famous, and he became a nationally acclaimed spokesperson for blacks. His new role would mean many hours of difficult work and travel. It would take him to the mansions of millionaires and to university campuses. He would be invited to the White House and the palace of the Queen of England. These opportunities helped Washington raise millions of dollars for education and job training at Tuskegee Institute.

In 1896, Washington was given an honorary **master's degree** from Harvard, the nation's oldest university. He had come a long way since his childhood as a poor slave who dreamed of one day learning to read.

Tuskegee teachers posed for the twenty-fifth anniversary of Tuskegee Institute. Washington is in the first row center, with his wife, Margaret, on his right.

Chapter Five

CRITICISM OF THE "ATLANTA COMPROMISE"

ore than a century after Washington's speech, some people still wonder whether the "Atlanta Compromise" helped or hurt the cause of equality for blacks. It is important to see the situation as Washington saw it at the time.

Booker T. Washington was born into slavery. To him, freedom itself was wonderful. He knew that blacks did not have equal rights. He believed that segregation was wrong. His first goal, however, was to see that blacks had basic necessities.

Washington felt it was more important to have food to eat than to eat with white people. It was more important for a black family to be able to

W. E. B. Du Bois nicknamed Washington the "Great Accommodator," implying that he did not stand up for blacks as much as he could have. Du Bois stated: "Mr. Washington represents in Negro thought the old attitude of adjustment and submission. . . . [His] programme practically accepts the alleged inferiority of the Negro races."

afford a home than to live in a white neighborhood. He believed that the opportunity to get a good education was more important than all races attending the same schools.

Washington's speech may have helped rebuild businesses in the South. Factories opened, cotton and steel mills were built, and railroads were modernized. The South began to prosper again.

Blacks, however, were not able to enjoy this prosperity. Segregation kept them from the best-paying work. In factories, they had the lowest-paying jobs. In cotton and steel mills, they could only work as janitors. On railroads, they were hired as porters, not as engineers or brakemen. Washington's famous compromise did not work out as he had expected, and some of his statements were held against him. Some blacks began criticizing Washington, arguing that he had been wrong to compromise.

One of these critics was W. E. B. Du Bois, a well-known black leader. His background was different than Washington's. He had been born in the North after the end of the Civil War and slavery.

W. E. B. Du Bois opposed Booker T. Washington's compromise with whites.

Du Bois argued that Washington had been wrong to compromise. He said segregation must not be tolerated, no matter what the cost.

Du Bois was well educated and had graduated from Fisk and Harvard universities. He argued that Tuskegee should be teaching academic courses instead of **vocational skills**. He believed this would create more highly educated leaders in the black community.

George Washington Carver taught Tuskegee students farming techniques for more than 40 years.

Washington still believed in his choices. In 1896, for example, Tuskegee had hired the first black graduate of Iowa State College. His name was George Washington Carver. For 47 years, Carver taught Tuskegee students and southern farmers how to grow bigger and better crops. He invented new uses for sweet potatoes and peanuts. He was given many awards for science, including one from President Franklin Roosevelt in 1939.

Still, criticism of Washington's ideas grew. A group of blacks formed a new organization in 1909 to work harder for civil rights. They named the group the National Association for the Advancement of Colored People (NAACP). Over time, the NAACP became very powerful. Du Bois was one of its leaders. He soon replaced Washington as the best-known spokesperson for blacks.

The NAACP is the nation's oldest civil rights organization. It held a key role in furthering the civil rights movement. Important members have included Martin Luther King Jr. and Rosa Parks.

Booker T. Washington with Andrew Carnegie (far right), William H. Taft (with hands folded), and R. C. Ogden (far left) at Tuskegee Institute's twenty-fifth anniversary in 1906

Chapter Six

IN TERMS OF HUMANITY

In 1901, Washington wrote his autobiography, *Up from Slavery.* One review called the moving story "one of the most cheerful, hopeful books that we have had the privilege to read."

Among the book's readers were wealthy northerners. Many of them had not thought much about the education of former slaves. Millionaires George Eastman, the camera maker, and Andrew Carnegie, the steel manufacturer, were among those impressed with Washington's story. After Eastman read the book, he sent Washington $5,000 to help with the education of blacks. Later Eastman would contribute $250,000 to the Tuskegee Memorial Fund. Carnegie gave Washington $600,000 for Tuskegee.

During that time, Washington was an adviser to President Theodore Roosevelt and received an invitation from the president to dine at the White House. Many southerners were shocked. Their segregation laws did not allow blacks and whites to eat together.

Segregation continued, however, with the next presidency. By 1911, President William Howard Taft began to remove nearly all blacks from government positions. When President Woodrow Wilson was elected in 1912, he continued to promote Taft's racist policies.

Throughout those presidencies, strict segregation was enforced in many branches of the U.S. government. For example, all blacks with jobs in the United States Postal Service were dismissed.

More than 1,000 blacks were killed because of their race in the South between 1900 and 1914. Good jobs were difficult for blacks to get. Segregation was still a fact of life. Washington began to believe that much more needed to be done.

He wrote a strongly worded article titled,

From speaking and traveling across the country, Washington became acquainted with wealthy men who had made their own way in life. Two of Washington's friends and contributors to his college were Henry H. Rogers, a key executive of Standard Oil, and Julius Rosenwald, president of Sears, Roebuck and Company.

EQUALITY

A drawing of President Roosevelt and Booker T. Washington dining at the White House while the South still had strict segregation laws.

"Is the Negro Having a Fair Chance?" In it, he argued against railroad segregation, lynchings, interference with the right of black men to vote, and the difficulty for blacks to receive education. Even Du Bois was pleased with Washington's frankness. As President Wilson's segregation practices continued, Washington spoke out against racism more strongly than ever.

By 1913, Washington realized that segregation had caused an increase in racism. Many blacks had received better educations and jobs because of his efforts. However, little progress had been made toward equality with whites.

Washington continued to work for black equality. He wrote a number of books and articles. He continued his work with the National Negro Business League, which he founded a decade earlier to encourage the

Booker T. Washington (sitting second from left) and other members of the National Negro Business League, around 1910

growth of black-owned businesses. Washington also continued to put much of his time and efforts into his beloved Tuskegee Institute.

By November 1915, Washington's health had declined. Many people said he was working himself to death. He was in New York making speeches and raising money for Tuskegee when he was hospitalized. After a week in the hospital, Washington realized he was dying.

Booker T. Washington continued speaking for civil rights until his death in 1915.

He and his wife took the train to Tuskegee that same afternoon, arriving home in the evening. "I was born in the South," said Washington. "I have lived and labored in the South. I expect to die in the South." He died the following morning, on November 14, 1915, at the age of 59.

As people around the country mourned his death, Washington was buried at Tuskegee. The United States had lost one of its most powerful and respected black leaders.

Booker T. Washington devoted his life to helping blacks improve their lives in a segregated United States. "More and more," he once said, "we must learn not to think in terms of race or color or political boundaries, but in terms of humanity."

TIME LINE

1856
Booker T. Washington is born in Virginia.

1865
The U.S. Civil War ends, and slaves are freed.

1866
Booker goes to school to begin his education.

1872
Booker leaves home to attend Hampton Institute, a three-year college for blacks.

1881
Washington begins teaching a class of 30 students at Tuskegee Institute in Alabama.

1895
Washington gives his speech, the "Atlanta Compromise," at the Cotton States and International Exposition.

1896
Washington is granted an honorary master's degree from Harvard University.

1899
Washington and his wife sail to Europe. He is invited to meet with the Queen of England.

1900
Washington organizes the National Negro Business League.

1901
Washington writes his autobiography, *Up from Slavery*. The book interests many wealthy northerners, who donate money to the Tuskegee Institute.

1903
President Theodore Roosevelt invites Washington to the White House to dine with him.

1909
W. E. B. Du Bois and other black leaders found the National Association for the Advancement of Colored People.

1911
President William Howard Taft begins racist policies that remove blacks from government jobs.

1915
Washington becomes ill. He dies on November 14 in Tuskegee, Alabama.

Glossary

Amendment
(uh-mend-munt)
An amendment is a change made to a law or legal document. The Thirteenth Amendment freed all slaves in the United States.

autobiography
(aw-toh-bye-og-ruh-fee)
An autobiography is when an author writes a book about his or her own life. Washington's autobiography is called *Up from Slavery.*

civil rights
(siv-il rites)
Civil rights are personal freedoms that belong to all citizens. While Washington was growing up, blacks were often denied their civil rights.

Confederate States of America
(kuhn-fed-ur-uht states of uh-mayr-uh-kuh)
The Confederate States of America are the Southern states that withdrew from the United States during the U.S. Civil War. The Confederate States of America formed when Booker was five years old.

discrimination
(diss-krim-i-nay-shun)
Discrimination is unfair treatment of people based on differences of race, gender, religion, or culture. Washington faced discrimination because he was black.

exposition
(ek-spoh-zih-shun)
A public show or exhibit is called an exposition. Washington gave his famous "Atlanta Compromise" speech at the Cotton States and International Exposition.

integration
(in-tuh-gray-shun)
Integration is the act of allowing different racial, class, or ethnic groups to be together in public facilities. Many blacks in the South supported the concept of integration.

master's degree
(mass-turs di-gree)
A master's degree is the educational degree that comes after a bachelor's degree. Washington earned an honorary master's degree from Harvard.

plantation
(plan-tay-shun)
A large farm, often in the South, is called a plantation. Booker's family worked on a plantation when he was young.

racism
(ray-sih-zum)
The belief that one race is superior to another is called racism. Washington faced racism from white Southerners.

secede
(sih-seed)
Secede means to officially withdraw from a group. Before the Civil War began, the South tried to secede from the United States in order to form its own country.

segregation
(seg-ruh-gay-shun)
Segregation is the act of keeping race, class, or ethnic groups separated. At the time of Washington's "Atlanta Compromise" speech, segregation was legal in the South.

slavery
(slay-vuh-ree)
Slavery is the practice of forcing a person or group of people to work for others without pay. Slavery was a common practice in the United States for nearly 250 years.

Union
(yoon-yun)
The Union refers to the states that stayed loyal to the U.S. government during the U.S. Civil War. The Union Army fought against the Confederate Army in the war.

vocational skills
(voh-kay-shun-ul skilz)
Skills that an individual can use at work are called vocational skills. Washington wanted Tuskegee students to learn vocational skills.

FURTHER INFORMATION

Books

Bolden, Tonya. *Portraits of African-American Heroes.* New York: Penguin, 2005.

Courtauld, Sarah. *Story of Slavery.* Tulsa, OK: EDC Publishing, 2008.

Hakim, Joy. *Reconstructing America.* New York: Oxford University Press, 2005.

McNeese, Tim. *Abolitionist Movement: Ending Slavery.* New York: Chelsea House, 2007.

Stanchak, John E. *Civil War.* New York: DK Publishing, 2000.

Washington, Booker T. *Up from Slavery: An Autobiography.* New York: Penguin, 2000.

Videos

Black History: From Civil War Through Today. St. Clair Vision, 2007.

A History of Black Achievement in America. Dir. Scott Gordon. Ambrose, 2005.

Web Sites

Visit our Web page for links about Booker T. Washington:

http://www.childsworld.com/links

NOTE TO PARENTS, TEACHERS, AND LIBRARIANS: We routinely verify our Web links to make sure they are safe, active sites—so encourage your readers to check them out!

INDEX

"Atlanta Compromise," 7, 19, 21
Atlanta, Georgia, 6, 17–18

Carnegie, Andrew, 24
Carver, George Washington, 23
civil rights, 19, 23
compromise, 19, 22–23
Confederate States of America, 9–10
Cotton States and International Exposition, 6, 17–18

Du Bois, W. E. B., 22–23, 26

Eastman, Andrew, 24
England, 20

Ferguson, Washington, 10

Hampton Institute, 10, 12–13, 15
Harvard, 20, 23

Integration, 7, 17

Jamestown, 9

King, Martin Luther, Jr., 23

Malden, West Virginia, 10, 13

National Association for the Advancement of Colored People (NAACP), 23
National Negro Business League, 26

Parks, Rosa, 23

Racism, 5, 26
Rogers, Henry H., 25
Roosevelt, Franklin, 23
Roosevelt, Theodore, 25
Rosenwald, Julius, 25

Segregation, 7, 18–19, 21–23, 25–27
self-reliance, 12, 14
slavery, 7, 8, 9, 10, 12, 21–22, 24, 26
South, 5–7, 8–10, 17–19, 22–23, 25, 27
speeches, 5–7, 18–20, 21–22, 26–27

Taft, William Howard, 25
Thirteenth Amendment, 9–10
Tuskegee, Alabama, 13, 14
Tuskegee Institute, 14–16, 20, 23, 27
Tuskegee Memorial Fund, 24

U.S. Civil War, 9, 17–19, 22
Union, 10
Up from Slavery, 24

Victoria (queen), 20
Virginia, 8–10
vocational skills, 23

Washington, Booker, Jr., 16
Washington, Booker T., childhood, 8–10
criticism of, 21–23
education, 10, 12
family, 16
speeches, 5–7, 17–20
work, 13–15, 24–27
Washington, Ernest, 16
Washington, Fannie (Smith), 16
Washington, Margaret, 16
Washington, Olivia (Davidson), 16
Washington, Portia, 16
White House, 20, 25
Wilson, Woodrow, 25, 26
Windsor Castle, 20